Tip$ on Tip$

Thriving in the Service Industry

Lee J. Bradshaw

At tipsontipsbook.com

Tip$ on Tip$

By Lee J. Bradshaw at www.tipsontipsbook.com
Copyright ©2011 Lee J. Bradshaw
First Edition: July 2011

Notice of Rights

Notice of Liability

About the Author

Lee is the father of thirteen children. He served in the U.S. Air Force, and has had numerous successful businesses since; two of which went nationwide in a matter of months. He has a vast amount of customer service experience contracting as a driver in the tourist industry. He has moved 68,000 customers in his driving career, and has 1,500,000 accident free miles. At present, Lee makes his home in Riverton, Utah with his wife, Cory. They are almost empty nesters with only seven children at home.

Lee J. Bradshaw can be contacted at Lee@tipsontipsbook.com

Acknowledgements

I would like to acknowledge foremost my Savior, who has set the perfect example for me to live a life of service. To him, I am forever grateful.

I am especially thankful to my wife, Cory, who also has been a great example to me, as well as to most all who come in contact with her. Even when I zigged when I should have zagged, she has always believed in me. I thank my children who make each day an adventure and make it all worthwhile. They fill my life with joy!

Foreword

The Secret of Working for Tip$

Witnessing bad customer service drives me crazy! With a little education, I believe "those in the service industry" can and will want to offer great, exceptional service.

In my career as a shuttle driver, I have moved 68,000 passengers and driven 1,500,000 miles. I have taken notes and constantly refined the how and the why of what I did.

I have to admit that I took my first job as a bridge until I found something better. I was told I could expect to bring home at least $1,600 a month. That first month I brought home over $3,000! In that company's history, nobody had ever done that. Those that choose to watch and learn what I was doing soon began to make more money than they had ever made. When I moved to a bigger company and applied these same principles, again I quickly rose to the top.

There were drivers that could see that what I was doing was worth learning. At the end of my thirteenth year, the company gave me an award that read *Most Improved*. At first, I was a little put off. I had always been proud to be recognized as the **#1 revenue earner"** every year. However, the owner of the company explained that I had taken the job to a whole new dimension: I had taught the other drivers my insights and philosophies, and the entire company had benefited in every way.

I promise you if you take service seriously, study and learn from my experience as well as your own interactions with customers. They will be valuable lessons in whatever endeavor you find yourself involved with later in your life.

P.S.

I have a really good memory and an attention to detail. These attributes can and should be acquired. They are as much a part of the "secret" as what you will learn from these stories.

Lee Bradshaw

Contents

My Philosophy on Gratuities

A Tip is purely personal. It is between my clients and me. I hate credit card tips that are determined before I have done anything. Also master bill tips that are determined by a group coordinator that most likely has never thrived in the trenches are very cold and impersonal.

I don't believe it is right for an employer to dip into an employee's tips. (If an employer wants honest, loyal, and trustworthy employees, stay out of the employees' pockets!) I've heard every angle and justification for *charging a percentage* back to the employee who earned the tip. Trust me, it will cost you in the end.

During my career in the service industry I have learned a lot that has helped me be successful in life and in businesses that I have owned.

I have moved Jimmy Buffet to Warren Buffet, and Martha Stewart to Carmen Electra. *Jimmy and*

Carmen are the better tippers. I have moved people from all over the world. I've seen people at their best, and sadly at their worst. I've moved millionaires, and people that didn't look like they had two dimes to rub together, from celebrities to *nobodies* and everybody in-between.

All these people had at least one thing in common, they were my customers, and I was blessed to serve them.

I felt that when they sat in my van, they deserved great service. It was my job to give the best that I had to offer and not to judge them for what they said, where they were from, what they were wearing, or who they were. Whether they were black, white, pink, blue, or polka-dotted my job was simply to offer them great service.

During my career I was privileged to move many interesting people and to work many exciting events. I was the Head Driver for Coca-Cola during the 2002 Winter Olympics. I have driven more than once for the Sr. PGA tour, and always looked forward to be included in the antics of Lee Trevino and Chi Chi Rodriguez. I remember the exact part of the highway I was driving on, the morning of Sept. 11th, 2001. These stories are meant to make you aware of people and the situations you will find yourself in. I hope that they help open your eyes to the possibilities of a life in the service industry.

For all of you that are not sure if this book is worth your time, or even if the service industry is for you, maybe these first two stories will help you decide.

Story #1 – Derrick the Derelict!

It was about three weeks into my eighth year. Derrick jumped into my van in the staging area at the airport. We both had a while to wait till our next ride. *(Waiting is something we all have to get used to if we plan on staying in the service industry).* Without so much as a hello, he asked me, "So, what's the secret?"

We all will have the experience to work with someone like Derrick. He was a new driver, and it didn't take long for his true colors to show. I had quickly noticed that he was a whiner and a cheat. Although he hadn't been around for long I had already seen him lie, cheat, and steal from the company, the clients, and the drivers. I had even given him a nickname, *Derelict.* The definition of derelict; *shamefully negligent in not having done what one should have done.*

In his eyes the company rules didn't apply to him. He complained if things didn't go his way, and he would do anything to get the advantage over the other drivers and customers.

Even though I knew this, I thought that maybe I could help him and maybe turn things around for him and all of those that had to deal with him. After all he was asking me for help.

"The Secret" I said back.

"Yeah, everybody says that you're the one to talk to." Then he added, "I haven't made a dime in tips."

I was shocked. I was already averaging over $100 a day in tips and the season hadn't even started.

Derrick was a college graduate; he had experience in hotel management. He had gloated the first few days that he was going to *school* all of us.

I started to tell him what I did and said to my passengers. First, I always knew what the snow conditions were and which resort had the best snow. If I noticed that they didn't have skis I would find out if they needed rentals. I knew the cheapest place for ski rentals, the place with the best equipment, the most convenient shop; that came right to the customers lodging, fitted them on site, and picked up the equipment at the end of the rental period. I knew who had the best steak, seafood, the most romantic, and the cheapest restaurant in town. If they were interested, I knew the history of the town and the state. I asked how their day was going and listened to their answers. I knew the best masseuse in town, and I had them on speed dial. Actually, I had everybody on speed dial. I started to tell Derrick more but he stopped me, he cut me off mid-sentence.

He yelled at me, **"YOU LET THEM USE YOUR PHONE?!! ALL THAT STUFF AIN'T MY !@#$% JOB!"** Then he jumped out of my van and slammed the door. Derrick quit about three weeks later. My average tips had climbed to about $200 a day.

Summary

In the service industry it is **all your job**. Being in the service industry is like being a small business owner without any of the risk.

When I started out, if I had a customer ask me a question that I didn't know the answer to, on my next day off I spent part of it researching for the answers. I hated to say, "I don't know." to the same question twice. I did the homework for my customers, finding the best Park City and Utah had to offer. I knew who was in town for concerts as well as the NBA schedule. I considered myself as the Concierge of Utah.

Derrick hated the service industry because he hated being of service. His tips reflected this. It is that simple. We've all had the waitress who hated her job. Think about it, did you enjoy the time spent at that restaurant, no matter what the occasion? How about the last time you bought tires? If the guy that *helped* you was rude, or even disconnected, how did you feel? Will you ever go back?

If this is you, there is no reason for you to go on. If you are a *Derelict*, do us all a favor and quit.

Story # 2 - Prayer

I hate to weed out readers so quickly but if this next story offends you, I am sorry.

Just after the second ski season, after I had switched companies, we had an end of the year party. I was awarded the *Top Dog* award, which basically meant I had made the company the most money, and since we all made the same commission percentage, it also meant that I had earned the most money.

After the award was given to me the three former *Top Dogs* cornered me, and demanded to know the *secret* to my success. I told them that my wife gathered my children three times a day, and they prayed for my success. Almost in perfect unison they said, "That's not it." and then turned and walked away in disgust.

Summary

Who you pray to is your choice. I'm OK with you not wanting to pray. Just don't force your will, not to pray, onto those that choose to. In the recent past it has been taboo to pray in public. I am glad to see a trend in the opposite direction.

I do not see this as a reason to force religion upon each other, but at the same time, forcing your will in the other direction isn't right either.

It also should be noted that these same three drivers were always right behind me in the #2, #3, or #4 positions without one prayer by them, or their families on their behalf. If that is the only difference between their positions and being #1, I hope I am never too proud to kneel down and ask for help, or have my family ask in my behalf.

Story # 3 – My First $100 Tip

It was a very cold night. It was my last run of the night, and I was tired.

My last passenger was a young lady from the University of Michigan. She had told her parents that she wasn't going to be able to make it to their annual family trip to Park City. All along she had planned to show up a day late to surprise them. It was her parent's 40th anniversary. She was very excited, but as we turned into the driveway of their Deer Valley estate, all the lights were off.

Before I unloaded her luggage I asked her to check to see if she could get in. As it so happened, all the doors were locked, and the door codes had been changed. I let her use my phone to call her parents, but nobody answered. So, we waited... Every so often she would tell me to leave her. She was sure someone would be home soon.

After waiting over an hour, I remembered on the way up the hill she had told me that it was her parents anniversary. I asked her if her parents had a favorite restaurant in Park City. They did. She told me it was Cicero's. I knew it well.

As we arrived at the restaurant she was sure they would be there, but I had her run in and make sure, while I waited. When she returned she was in tears. They weren't there.

We sat in front of the restaurant for a minute to regroup. Then I remembered that a new fancier Italian restaurant had just opened just up the hill and across the street. Again I waited outside, but this time it was her father that came out in tears. He pulled me from the van and hugged me. It was almost embarrassing. He couldn't believe someone could be so dedicated.

He was very thankful that I hadn't left his daughter along the road somewhere, even when she had asked to be. He paid me for the extra time, and tipped me my first $100.

Every year after that he asked the reservation agent

for me when he came into or left town, and he always had the same tip for me. I probably transported the guy, or one of his family members a dozen times, and he always had a crisp new $100 bill for me even though it never was as hard to complete the job.

Summary

The math is pretty simple, $1,300 in tips for going above and beyond one time. Doing my best and treating a young lady like I hope my daughter would be treated, doesn't seem like that is so hard to figure out.

Listening is always a good thing. It may help you do your job. Never *cut bait and run*. One day you will find yourself in a tough situation. Be grateful for the experience. These experiences, good or bad, can never be taken away from you and should be looked at as tips as much as the cash.

Story # 4 – My First Billionaire

I picked up this gentleman from Stein Erickson's lodge at the top of Deer Valley. I believe he was one of the keynote speakers at a conference there. He told me that he needed me to be as quiet as possible because he had a very important business call to make while we were on the way to the airport. He gave me all the details that I needed to get him to where he needed to be dropped off before he started the call.

As we started down the mountain it started to snow heavily. By the time we hit I-80 less than ten minutes later, it was a whiteout, and at least a foot of snow was already on the road. As we proceeded down the mountain my client finished his first call in which he had purchased 6 brand new Boeing 767's.

He commented on my driving skills and how safe I made him feel. Next he informed me that he had one more call to make, and again asked me to be as quiet as possible. During the next call the roads got more and more treacherous.

An eighteen-wheeler passed me on the right going much too fast as we were approaching a very sharp curve. I knew before the truck driver knew what was going to happen.

As he started to jackknife I slowed down and changed lanes over to the left as far as possible. The truck just missed us as it lost control and crossed over into our lane right in front of us. I then calmly crossed over to the far right lane as the truck crashed into the center divider. My client let out a barely audible whimper as we passed through the huge cloud of snow unharmed. There was a huge pile-up on the highway behind us as the debris from the truck and trailer covered all three lanes of traffic.

While all this was happening, he was on a conference call with Delta Airlines leasing them the 6 new Boeing aircrafts he had just purchased ten minutes earlier.

When we arrived at the airport he hung up, and told me he had never seen driving as smooth, and he was amazed that I'd done it during the worst conditions he'd ever been in. He also said that he would never have been able to do it himself, and **"that he owed me his life!"** Then he shook my hand profusely, then he hugged me, and then he handed me a crisp $1 bill.

Summary

When this happened I was speechless. I'm sure terminal services had to tell me to move along, and they probably helped me pick my jaw off the ground. I did everything right. I do not know what else I could have done in this situation.

I do know that the wrong thing to do would have been to chase the guy down, turn him upside down, and shake him. I may have felt like it, but it is never the right thing to do. Never *beat up your customer* (physically or verbally). The best response is always to smile and say "Thank you."

Story # 5 – High and Dry

I had dropped off my passengers, and noticed in the shadows of the parking lot a pile of luggage. As I investigated, a family of four was also standing in the darkness. I asked if I could help, and they told me that this was where they had reservations, so their driver had dropped them off, but they could not find the lobby. I knew that this property did not have an onsite check-in, so I piled them in my van, and took them to the check-in location. I waited for them as I did for all my guests. Then took them back to their lodging, as I did for all my guests. I helped them carry their luggage up to their room, and made sure that the key worked, as I did for all my guests. They were embarrassed that they didn't have more than ten dollars for a tip. I assured them that it was a fine tip, and thanked them for the chance to serve them. Before I left I gave them a card for our company.

Summary

Five days later another driver for our company handed me an envelope. He informed me that a family of four that he had taken to the airport earlier that morning had made him promise that he would get it to me. As I opened it, the other driver's jaw hit the ground. In it was a note that said, "Thank You. We called the company that was supposed to take care of us a few nights ago and demanded that we get a refund. We thought it was only right that you should get this money." Along with the note was $118.

Story # 6 – Bringing Home an Axe Murderer

Again it was late, and during the Sundance Film Festival (the busiest week of the year). I had a van full of people all going to different places. One of my passengers had traveled all the way from India. He said he didn't remember where he was staying, so I proceeded to drop off the rest of my passengers. When I was done he confessed that he had traveled all the way to Park City, Utah from India without making any plans for accommodations.

We stopped by at least a dozen hotels, and called another dozen or more to no avail. Every bed in town was full. My dispatcher had gone home and given me an early morning start time over the radio. My passenger suggested that I drop him off at the nearest 7-11 and he would be happy.

That is when I called home to check with my wife to make sure that it was OK to offer him our couch. She said it was all right as long as he wasn't an axe murderer. I assured her that he hadn't traveled half way around the world to kill his shuttle driver and his family. When we arrived home I found that we already had a house full of guests. My mother-in-law and one of my sisters-in-law were also staying the night. They had the couch made into a bed for our Indian guest. The next morning I found that my mother-in-law had stayed up all night talking to him. They became great friends and corresponded for years until my mother-in-law passed away a few years back.

Summary

In thirteen years and over 68,000 passengers, I only brought home passengers twice. The other time was a beautiful young lady that was meeting friends, but had no idea where they were staying. This time I had to convince her that I wasn't the axe murderer. Again I called my wife, and she convinced her that it was safe.

Both situations ended pretty much the same. With much needed sleep and a new day, we figured it all out as soon as we arrived back in Park City the next morning. I wouldn't want my daughter or brother sleeping on the floor at 7-11 only to wake up in a strange town with no resources.

And for the record, both times I was tipped very well. I have been told that Indians and pretty girls never tip. I have found that when treated well, they do.

Story # 7 – Irate Passenger #6,798

I was told I could go home for the night, but when I was almost home I heard the airport dispatcher frantically calling for a van. I called the dispatcher, told him where I was, and how long it would take me to get to him.

After I had given my ETA (estimated time of arrival), I realized that I needed to get fuel. I called the dispatcher back and told him of my mistake. I asked the dispatcher to ask if the passenger would like me to pick him up first, then he could pick up his "beverage of choice" at my expense while I fueled. The dispatcher refused to simply ask the passenger this, he told me to fuel as quickly as possible, and then return to the airport.

When I finally arrived my passenger was furious. I let him vent. I took responsibility for everything that had gone wrong with his day. From his corn flakes being soggy that morning, to our company running out of vehicles that night, and of course, the fact that

I had to fuel.

It didn't take him long to see that I was trying to be part of the solution not part of the problem.

That's when he asked if it would be possible to stop for a drink. I laughed out loud as I pulled off the same exit, and then pulled into the same station that I had fueled at just a few minutes earlier.

In the end he apologized for his temper tantrum, and paid his bill with an extra $100 included.

Summary

I learned to love the irate passenger. I love the irate passenger so much so that at the beginning of each year I would make it a point to walk into the airport, introduce myself to the new staff, and tell them that if they ever had an irate passenger **I wanted them**. I found that if I could turn them they were almost always great tippers. None of the other drivers wanted them and would rather I pull around them in the line up.

I also wasn't afraid to tell a client that I had made a mistake and let them in on the decision-making process. Clients are much happier if they are informed and asked for their input.

I also knew that I only made money when my wheels were turning, so I always thought waiting around for a better load was stupid.

Story # 8 – Missed Opportunity

First of all, I have to admit this is not my story. It is from a close friend, and it is the story of his biggest sale. He works at a jewelry store where they worked on a rotation basis.

The sales lady at the front of the line was disappointed when the next customer through the door, *her customer*, was an old farmer still in his overalls and mucking boots.

Seeing her dismay, my friend offered to *take this one*. With a sigh of relief, she agreed. Within minutes my friend found out that this gentleman was just turning fifty and had never bought himself anything. So my friend started with the biggest ring in the store, which the man loved and bought on the spot.

Not only did my friend make the biggest commission possible, but also the ring had a bonus attached that made him even more money that day. He broke a quota for that week which made him another bonus. My friend makes three commissions for that one sale.

Summary

Take what is given. Make the most out of it. Maybe it is being put before you because you have something to learn. Or maybe it is a blessing in disguise.

I am sure the sales lady that missed this opportunity and prejudged this man is still whining about how she was robbed by my friend! If this is you, get over it, and learn from your mistakes.

Story # 9 – Everything Right

I arrived early to pick up a family. I knocked on the door, and told them that I was there but not to rush because I was early. As I was waiting, I tidied up my van. I had bottled water, and had even stopped and bought some donuts. One by one my passengers brought their luggage out, and I loaded it up. Then to my surprise, they came out, loaded up, and we were on the road fifteen minutes early.

They were very thankful for the donuts and water, and asked to listen to some classic rock on the radio. Everyone was singing along and having a great time. As we rolled into the airport, the father of the group thanked me, and said that the ride was the perfect end to a great vacation. When we unloaded them every member of the family shook my hand and thanked me. Then they all disappeared into the terminal leaving me with nothing but an empty donut box and used water bottles.

Summary

I have to admit, when you get stiffed and especially after you've done everything right it bothers you. In this instance I was left shaking my head.

I was cleaning out my van on the curb when I heard a light knock on the side of the van. It was the father of the group with a tip in his hand, visibly embarrassed that he had forgotten.

Too many times I have seen other drivers yell at passengers when they sensed that they were going to get stiffed. It never turns out well. At best, the passenger will give up a dollar or two, and that is probably more than they deserve. If they decide to yell at their customers will those same customers come back and surprise them.

Story # 10 – What's in a Name

The first company I worked for called all the drivers by their first names or a nickname. When I first started they already had a *Lee* working for them. One of the veteran drivers saw that I had a natural knack for making my passengers feel comfortable. In so doing the tips flowed easily. It was that veteran driver that started calling me *Tip* or *Tip the Driver*. The name stuck, and it seemed that all the drivers liked it when the dispatcher called *Tip the Driver* over the radio for all the passengers to hear.

Summary

I'm sure this nickname has helped me over the years. The second company called their drivers by a number. It was very cold and impersonal. The other drivers, and dispatchers would slip my old nickname in every once in a while.

Be careful in the nickname that is attached to you. Nobody wants *Crash or Pokey* as his or her driver.

Story # 11 – The Value of Good Service

The company I drove for flew me and another driver down to L.A. to pick up two vans. On the way home, Terry begged me to stop in Las Vegas with him so he could check out the newest sports bar in town. It boasted to have put millions into this new restaurant and bar. No other sports bar was supposed to have as many or as big and giant plasma high definition screens.

I have to admit the place was very impressive. Huge HD TV's were everywhere. We didn't have any particular game that we wanted to watch so we let them seat us anywhere.

Soon after we were seated, there was quite a stir as tables were rearranged, and at least eighteen huge football players came in.

As they were being seated the leader of the group said to the host, "We are from the University of Tennessee and U of T is playing BYU in fifteen minutes. Is this table close to where you are going to be showing that game?"

At once the host pulled a list out of his pocket, looked it over and said "We are not showing that game tonight." Then he turned and walked away.

I am not sure who was more shocked, the leader of that group or me. He walked to the center of the table, informed the rest of the party that he was going to the liquor store, and then back to his room to watch the game and order pizza. He told them why, and they all filed out of the restaurant behind him.

Summary

WOW! My dinner cost me over $40, without alcohol, appetizer, dessert, or a tip.

These guys were there to watch an entire football game (i.e. three or four hours as their customers).

My best guess is that this host cost the restaurant over $1,000 in seconds, not to mention at least a $200 tip for the server and bartender, maybe even more. I was surprised how fast it had all happened. There was no time for the manager or owner to do any damage control. Terry and I were left there with our mouths gaping wide open, looking at each other, and then to the empty table.

As the host, what would you have done?

I would have whipped the list from my back pocket (just like the other host did), upon seeing that the game wasn't on the schedule I would have informed them of the fact, but **assured them that I was there to work for them.** I would have talked to the owner/manager, and made arrangements to put that game on the biggest screen possible.

Even if the owner/manager hated the U of T, I can assure you he wouldn't want that kind of money walking out of his establishment—especially in a sports bar where excited, happy customers lead to more excited, happy customers. The monetary loss of that one incident is impossible to know.

I hope the ESPN sports bar at the New York, New York in Las Vegas, Nevada has learned from this oversight.

Story # 12 – The Rewards of Integrity

After dropping off a couple at the airport I checked in with the dispatcher and asked to go for fuel.

While I was fueling, the dispatcher called me and asked me to check the seats for a diamond earring that one of my passengers was missing. When I opened the back door, there in the tracks of the door was the biggest diamond I'd ever seen.

I called back that I had found it and told him to tell the passenger that I'd be right there and where he could meet me.

Upon arrival back at the airport I found the worried and anxious passenger. He thanked me and gave me another $20 tip and ran to catch up with his wife and his flight.

Summary

The other drivers, my supervisor, and sadly the owner of the company mocked me. They couldn't believe that I hadn't kept the diamond.

Two weeks after this happened. I walked into the office and was greeted by the accountant of the company. She congratulated me for a job well done and for representing the company in such a positive way. The drivers and dispatchers did the same.

I was directed to the bulletin board where there was a thank you note along with a newspaper article that the owner of the diamond earring had written in her local newspaper in Georgia about her experience. She raved about our company and her driver.

Sadly the owner came in and made a comment that shocked me. Again he made the comment that the diamond must have been very valuable, and that I was stupid for returning it. He did this right in front of all his staff in whom he expected to be honest and trustworthy employees.

That night when I arrived at home, my wife asked me whom I knew in Georgia. She handed me an envelope, which had a Thank You note that told me of the family heirloom that I was responsible for returning. Along with this note was a check for $500. Two weeks after that our local paper ran the same article.

Just because you work around people with no integrity doesn't mean you shouldn't have some yourself.

In the end you will be blessed.

Story # 13 – The Kiss of Death

For the first half of my career there were six words I absolutely hated to hear. One little phrase that always ended in disappointment–not just for me but I believe it to be industry-wide.

"I'll make it worth your while."

It never ended up worth my while. Then I realized that I needed to speak up. From then on I jokingly would say to that passenger,

"Before we make a deal like that, first you need to know what my while is worth."

Then I would tell them what I was averaging an hour that day, and they would know what I expected. They could decide if it was worth it to them.

After I started telling my passengers what my *while was worth* I never had a problem when my passengers made that statement.

Summary

Most of the drivers thought I was being overly bold. My thinking was, when a guest asks you for extra service with a promise to compensate you for your effort, a negotiation process has started.

Before I started doing this I would save my clients money, some times hundreds of dollars, while losing money for myself in commissions and tips. Some times the loss on my part would be in the hundreds of dollars.

My friend Chris was one of the unbelievers until this last year. With this story is fresh in his ears, he went to work only to have his first passengers of his day say these dreaded words. I guess he was finally tired enough of the disappointment that he finally used my line. He was amazed that his client wasn't offended at all and paid him an extra fifty dollars for his time.

Story # 14 – Do You Know Who I Am

Almost as annoying as *I'll make it worth your while* is this phrase: *Do you know who I am?* If they have to ask, the answer is either NO or I don't care. If I had a nickel for every time I've heard that one, I'd have a lot of nickels.

Everybody deserves great service. Even the self-absorbed celebrities deserves great service, but, not at the expense of others. I have seen service providers time and time again forget this simple truth. Chasing a perceived *Big Tip* at the expense of the *Average Joe.*

Summary

If my passengers paid extra for a private ride I always provided them with the best I had to offer, no matter who they were.

If they were in a shared ride van, everyone on the van paid the same amount for the same service. I still offered each passenger the same great service, but I came to realize when someone was asking this they were asking me to let down my standard for everyone else on the van but them.

In the beginning, I let people intimidate me. Sadly most of this happened during the Sundance Film Festival. Every year Park City hosts the film festival. To be honest, some of the people that attend can be the rudest people in the world.

I soon realized that communication and knowledge were the best way to defuse these guests.

I would tell the passenger who was making the unreasonable demands that we offered private vans, cars, and limo's. It was often too late for them to make any changes for that trip, but they could be more prepared the next time instead of trying to bully the next driver they came in contact with.

If you take the opportunity to educate and enlighten all your guests, especially those that are disgruntled or confused, it will help everyone involved, even if they are not involved until the next time.

Some of the time it would be too late to salvage any relationship with the guest that made the unreasonable demands, but the other guests usually could see that I was working for the good of all the guests in my charge, and they usually made up for the one that was disgruntled.

Story # 15 – Take Credit for Everything

Since we are talking Sundance, here is another Sundance story.

I had a load of seven passengers scattered around town. It was a very busy hour and all the other vans were completely full. I had the only three available seats. My passengers were skiers, but they were talking amongst themselves, and lightly complaining that they hadn't seen any celebrities during their stay.

Just then, the dispatcher called me and asked if I could pick up three more passengers. I said that I could, and it turned out the new passengers were just a few driveways away from where we were.

I pulled in front of the lobby and no one was around. I waited for a while and still no one came. I still had one of my original passengers to pick up, so I got back into the van and drove up the road to gather him. Just as I left the driveway my dispatcher called and asked if I had left my new passengers. I told him what I was doing and that they would have to be ready when I came back.

When I returned, John Malkovich and Dennis Hopper were standing there, bags in hand apologizing for not being ready when I came by the first time.

Along with them was a Prima Donna that oozed attitude before I even opened the doors to the van. She was appalled that our company had sent her a shared ride van.

I guess that she thought that our company should have a private vehicle standing by for her at a moment's notice.

She refused to get in the van. I explained that these seats were the last in Park City, and she could take them or leave them. Dennis and John said that they would be happy to take them.

Then she turned her attention to the seats that were occupied in the first row. I explained that the three seats I had were in the back, but she just glared at the people in *her* seats.

John broke the tension and as he headed toward the van he said he would be happy to sit in the back, but our lady just stared until the couple in the seat finally said they would be delighted to sit in the back with Mr. Malkovich.

Then Mr. Hopper almost picked up the *lady* and tossed her in our van.

Summary

As we rolled out of town I reminded my original seven passengers about their complaint. Not only did they see a celebrity, I now was providing a ride with at least two celebrities!

Story # 16 – Don't get Bored

I definitely had reason and opportunity to let boredom seep in. After a million and a half miles and 68,000 passengers it is a possibility. But more importantly, I used it to my advantage. On the thirty-five mile trip to Park City we would climb about three thousand feet in elevation.

I learned through observing my passengers that twice during the trip we would pass a point where their ears would pop. I observed it so many times that I started telling the people that their ears where about to pop about ten seconds before they would. Many of them would start tell me there was no way for me to know that information. Before they could get one word out of their mouths their ears would pop.

Even better, if I had a fussy baby on board I would warn the parents so that they could give the baby a bottle or pacifier before that spot on the trip up the mountain.

Summary

All the useless info that you gather day by day is only useless if you never use it.

My passengers felt like I cared for their well-being. And I did. I think that it also felt like a magic trick, or I was predicting the future. It was amazing how much credibility I had after using this simple gesture. With practice it took very little effort.

Story # 17 – It Never Hurts to Have a Beautiful Young Lady on Board

I had ten passengers leaving the airport to Park City. There were nine men from Atlanta and a lady from New Orleans.

As we headed up the hill I found out that the guys were big game hunters that had traveled all over the country to hunt. So I started to point out deer, elk, and moose.

At first they were all having a hard time seeing what I was seeing. Then I told the young lady to look for the horizontal lines up in the brush. Wham!!! As soon as she knew what to look for she was on fire.

For the rest of the trip she was finding game everywhere. The men could not believe she could find the big game faster than they could.

Before the end of the trip they all had offered to pay her way on their next hunting trip, two of them proposed before we reached Park City.

All the men tipped me very well, but the woman along with a tip thanked me for such an unexpected and unforgettable trip and a new way to impress a man.

Summary

This is another instance of taking credit for the cards that you are dealt. Also as I write this I am reminded that almost without thinking about it I found ways on every trip to engage my clients. I found common ground or something of interest to talk about. It is amazing to me how my passengers and I could have a long meaningful conversation that was started off by a innocent comment about shoes, the color of someone's hair or eyes, etc.

I have ridden with drivers that don't say a word to their passengers, barely even a Thank You when they do receive a gratuity. Then they wonder why they aren't receiving the same amount as I am.

Invest time, energy, and anything else that is needed or comes to mind. Take responsibility for their well-being and for your own take-home pay.

Story # 18 – Be Aware

Beware. Utah is full of wildlife. Not every trip resulted in us seeing a moose or a herd of elk.

If I ever said anything about showing my passengers wildlife it was a disaster. We would see nothing, and everybody was disappointed.

If I let it flow, then when I saw something and pointed it out, it was always better.

On one trip I was busy pointing out all the wildlife, but the lady up front wasn't seeing anything. Finally, she couldn't take it anymore. She called me a liar, and said there was no way I could see all these animals and drive at the same time. So I pulled the van over and pointed out a huge moose (as big as a Clydesdale) less than one hundred yards away.

At first she saw nothing, then with a little education on what to look for she finally saw it. She was one of the happiest and excited passengers I had ever had.

Summary

Are you starting to see a pattern here? Your clients don't owe you anything. You are providing a service, usually one that they have already paid for. A tip is an added bonus for you by them for great, over the top service. I love people and being of service.

You should too.

Be aware of the signals that your clients give you. Either subtle or in your face, take responsibility each and every time. If you slip up and miss an opportunity, learn from your mistakes and do better next time.

Story # 19 – – The Best in People

I drove a lot of different personalities over the years. The most touching period was definitely during the 9/11 attacks. Airlines were grounded, and no one knew when they would start flying again. I watched the anguish and worry in peoples faces.

For the most part, people were understanding with one another. People listened to each other's stories and hugged each other at the end of the trip. Sadly, I took some people to the Airport three or four times before they were actually able to find a flight out. I felt the most for the people that were trying to get back to their homes in New York City. The phone lines were jammed, and it was impossible for some of them to get hold of anyone from home for status reports.

During that time people were truly good to one another, and if someone had a bad day everyone forgave them and allowed them to vent.

Summary

While this was all going on I stopped excepting tips offered by my passengers. We did not know how long everyone would be stuck. People were truly grieving and overcome with worry. I would hope that every one that chooses to work in this industry could learn to back away and not chase a stupid dollar from someone in a traumatic situation.

It was during this tragedy that I went to work for my passengers, in a different way. I lobbied with my boss that we should stop charging passengers over and over again. Passengers had to ride with us back and forth, day after day. No one knew when the airports would open again.

One grief stricken man, that had an office in one of the twin towers, rode with me four days back and forth trying to get a flight out. I'll never know what he found or lost that day. Hopefully, I gave him less to worry about when he was in my care.

Story # 20 – Deal with the Devil

I used to own a detail business. We specialized in big rigs (eighteen wheelers). One day a truck driver called in over the CB radio and made an appointment to have his truck detailed.

His handle was *The Tasmanian Devil*.

It was a big job. He wanted the works. When he arrived we bid the job, and he agreed to the price.

He informed us that we had four hours to complete the job. He had an appointment to pick up a load, and we needed to be done at that time. We assured him the work could be done in the time allowed.

As soon as the driver left, my brother and I went to work. I finished my side of the truck in record time, but when I went to the other side of the truck my brother was still working on the first fuel tank (our specialty was to polish the aluminum fuel tanks so that they looked like chrome).

My brother showed me that there was a problem with

the tank he was working on. As he polished it, it would look great until the very last step, then as he finished up a shadow would appear.

I hurried and finished the rest of the truck while he tried over and over again to make it look as good as the rest of the truck.

When the driver arrived to pick up his truck at the appointed time he was very happy with all but the one fuel tank.

I quickly grabbed the buffing wheel and tried one more time but to no avail.

Taz reached for his wallet and asked for a discount. I asked him if he was happy. He said he was, all except that one tank. So, I shocked him, my brother, and myself a little. I told him if he wasn't happy I couldn't charge him.

He argued that the two of us had spent most of a day detailing his truck, and he had to pay us something. I told him that on his next trip through Salt Lake City he could stop by, and let us have another chance to make his tank look as good as the rest of the truck.

I almost had to throw my brother in our truck, and then we drove away.

Summary

I read a book a few years back called *Raving Fans*.

This story could be called *Raving Disgruntled Customers*. Taz talked about us clear across the country. Over the CB he told driver after driver about how we had worked all day long and not charged him a dime because of the one flaw.

Soon after that we had a driver come into our shop that had heard about us while driving in Pensacola, Florida and another from New York City, NY. He came back later and let us fix that tank and paid us in full.

For years drivers came in and said that Taz had told them that if you were going to have your truck detailed, *Popeye Brothers* out of SLC, UT was the only place to have it done.

The band, *Guns & Roses,* was the biggest show on the road with thirteen 18-wheelers and three motor coaches. Sure enough Taz told them about us, and when they came through town they had us detail and polish all their aluminum. That is a lot of wheels and tanks, and of course all of those customers told other drivers clear across the country about our shop.

We owed it all to one guy we did not charge because he was not 100% happy.

I have to admit; when I didn't charge him it was so he didn't complain over the CB radio while he was close by. I had no idea of the ripple effect that it would cause.

I hope it is a lesson I never forget.

Story # 21 – Dancing for Dollars

I picked up ten ladies that had been forgotten about by another company. They were visibly upset and rightly so.

I quickly loaded them up, and I hurried down the mountain as quickly and as safely as possible. I joked all the way with them and told my stories. When we arrived at the airport. I jumped out of the van and started unloading the luggage.

 Out of the corner of my eye I saw the ladies one by one starting to sprint to the terminals.

Then to my surprise, I felt a hand in my pocket. All of the ladies were coming back, and since my hands were full of luggage they were leaving tips in my pockets.

I joked with them to at least wait for the music, so I could dance for them. They all were laughing as they frantically ran for their flights.

Summary

In times of stress I have found that a little lighthearted fun and playfulness eases the pain and tension of a bad situation. Be careful not to cross that fine line though.

I have found never to point blame or make fun of another provider. It would have been an easy target to focus on the misstep of the company that forgot these ladies. Instead I focused on the fact that I had the chance to provide these ladies with great service, and if the misstep hadn't happened I wouldn't of had the opportunity to meet such sweet, beautiful, and intelligent young looking, over sixty year old women.

Shortly after I dropped off these ladies I received a surprise phone call from the owner of the competing transportation company. He had already received numerous calls from his guests raving about how I had treated them and the fact that I had not badmouthed his company. Even the event coordinator got involved and called me to thank me for my efforts. Both the owner and event coordinator sent a bonus check to me with a thank you note for a job well done.

Story # 22 – Influencing Others

One year I noticed that the tips from a particular hotel were down drastically. Our passengers from that Hotel were always complaining that we were late and visibly upset.

I also had noticed that one of the bellman, let's call him Chris, was definitely disgruntled and treated all of the drivers from our company poorly.

So, one morning on my way up the hill I decided to stop by to pay Chris a visit. I made a quick stop at Starbucks and picked him up a coffee and donut. When I arrived I offered him my peace offering, and I asked to talk to him privately for a minute.

We walked out of earshot of any one, and I asked him why he had such a bad attitude towards the company I worked for.

As it turned out, his girl friend worked for the competition and out of loyalty to her he hated us.

I then asked him how his year was going *tip wise*. He

confided that it wasn't turning out to be one of his worst years.

I told him my perspective on his situation, which was, he worked at a beautiful hotel. It was usually the first one we came to as we came into town. So, obviously it was one of the last ones we came to on our way out of town.

The policy of our company was to start picking up passengers at the top of the hour and if we had pick-ups throughout town it would sometimes be half past the hour before we made our last pickup at his hotel, but it was only a half hour to the airport from there. So we could still get the passengers to the airport in time.

I told him to try this. When he was helping his guest get ready for departure to help them stay positive.

I added it was my experience that a negative customer tended not to tip anyone. So if he were focused on ruining my day *tip wise* it would surely affect *him tip wise.*

In my eyes his guests were the luckiest in all Park City; they dropped off first and picked up last. In other words their vacations started first and ended last.

I left him to think about what I had said. Before the week was over he pulled me aside and thanked me. By learning from my perspective and applying it with his guests his tips had gone through the roof.

After Chris saw how quick and effective my simple *words of wisdom* were to put in effect, and how much of an impact it had on his income, he was eager to share them with the entire hotel staff. My investment paid off in my behalf as well. I noticed my tips rising immediately after our conversation, from the guests from that one hotel.

Summary

Any time you try to affect someone else's income by bad mouthing or negatively influencing others I have found that it affects you more. Your attention to the important things, like your customers, is diverted.

Besides, happy customers are better tippers. If you spend any time focusing on any negative aspect it is time spent taking your clients in the wrong direction, to use a driving metaphor. That means you are further from getting any tip for yourself.

If another company's service is really that bad they won't be around for long. There is no reason for you to point out the mistakes of others.

Here is an exercise; hold your hand out and point across the room. Now look at the inside of your hand. What do you see? Three fingers pointing back at yourself.

What this exercise teaches me is to be careful when pointing out the shortcomings of others. Three times the focus will be on me if I fall into this trap.

Story # 23 – The Real Santa

One of the weirdest tips that I ever received was during the Christmas season.

At the end of a run as I was unloading my last passenger he asked me if I'd like to make a hundred dollar tip. "Sure I would." was my answer, "But what do I have to do?" I said a little sheepishly.

He assured me it was nothing illegal. He told me that he had noticed the picture of my family in the van and wanted to give them a present. He handed me one hundred fifty dollars. I was confused. He told me to take the money, spend all of it, and bring him the receipts.

If I did as I was told he would give me a $100 dollar tip. That night after my shift I went shopping, bought gifts for my kids, and made sure that I kept the receipts.

The next morning I felt a little silly as I headed up the mountain to start my day. How was I going to track down this guy to give him the receipts? I felt sheepish even thinking about having the front desk ring his room to finish this deal.

I decided that he had already given me $150, and that was very generous. I didn't plan on bothering him any further.

To my surprise, my first pick up of the morning was at the hotel where I had dropped off the *little elf* the night before. It was early in the morning, so I thought there would be no way I'd see him there.

Unexpectedly, as I was loading the luggage, he appeared behind me and tapped me on the shoulder. He asked if I had the receipts. I pulled them from my wallet and gave them to him, and he handed me another $100 bill.

Summary

This is still one of my family's favorite Christmas stories. I am not sure what the *moral* of the story is though.

This is a good time to point out one of my philosophies.

As a driver we all run the risk of just being a *back of a head*. No personality, and nothing to remember you by. If you don't connect with your customers it is easy for them to forget you. So one of the ways I became a *real person* was to have a picture of my family staring back at them.

As my family grew, I was surprised at the number of people who asked about the new baby or even remembered my children's names. I believe our customers want to connect to us. We should be warm and approachable. And if they want to buy my children a Christmas gift, who am I to argue.

Story # 24 – Even I Almost Make Mistakes

This is said tongue in cheek. Of course I have blown it more than once.

This story is about a couple that rode with me more than once, and every time they had stiffed me.

I noticed them as soon as they walked out of the terminal. I had moved them at least six times in my career, and they had stiffed me every time. So, as I drove up the mountain I rehearsed what I *needed* to say to them. The closer I got to their address the madder I got, and the more passionate I became about my up coming monologue.

Just when I was about to unleash my wrath upon them, the gentleman handed me a very large tip. As he did he leaned close to me and whispered that on the way up the hill he had realized that he had never tipped the drivers that had brought him to and from Park City. It had never occurred to him until that night that we *worked* for tips.

He was very gracious and thankful.

Summary

As a service provider our job is very simple. We provide service. In this relationship our customers don't have a *job*. They are the **customers.** If they expect their grapes to be peeled while you fan them with ostrich feathers and rub their feet, and this is the quality of service your company offers, then start peeling or go home.

It would also be nice if you went the extra mile and added your own personal touch to the service that you provide. Like a bowl of ice because I love my peeled grapes chilled, and don't touch my feet.

Also, I would like to tell you all about one of my other philosophies. More than half way though my driving career this philosophy changed. What I am talking about is showing my tips. In the beginning I was afraid to. I didn't want to flaunt them and I never did. Around my eighth or ninth season I started putting the tips that I had just received in the cup holder. I was surprised how fast my tips went up.

I started testing this and started only putting *fives* then *tens* and then *twenties* in the cup holder as I would get back in the van after dropping off a passenger. All the other passengers were watching me more than I had realized.

Each time I raised the bar my passengers would rise up to it.

One day I gave a ride up the mountain to two families. Both men were lawyers. After unloading the first family at their hotel the father of the group asked me if I had change for a hundred dollar bill. I did, and asked him how he wanted it back. He told me to just give him fifty, and we'd call it even.

When I jumped back into the van, out of habit I put the bill into the cup holder.

It was another ten-minute ride to the other family's hotel. As we proceeded down the road I realized what a valuable tool this was. Every few seconds the lawyer in the front seat leaned over ever so slightly to get a better angle to look at that bill. He even reclined his seat.

After I had unloaded him and his family, he handed me a crisp new $100 bill.

Now I know that showing your tips isn't for everyone, but back to this story. The guy that had never tipped me, this gentleman and his wife had rode with me over and over again. It wasn't until I started showing my tips that he finally realized that I worked for tips. It was then, when he saw the money, that he started tipping.

Story # 25 – Even A Clown Can do it

Here is one more story along this same line of thinking.

Andrea owns an entertainment company. She is a great clown and also dresses up as other characters. She does singing telegrams, balloon animals, and face painting parties.

She asked me for some pointers on how to bring in more money to her business. One of the simplest things I suggested was to put a dollar in her breast pocket of her costume with part of the bill hanging out.

She was amazed that without saying a word she now has started getting tips.

And now at her higher end parties she leaves a five hanging out of the pocket, and again she is excited that her tips have gone through the roof.

Summary

In this instance I reminded Andrea that the dollar bill needed to barely be visible, almost subliminal. When we were talking about this I told her to treat it as an experiment. And like all good experiments, to continue to make slight adjustments, and to document what worked and what did not.

I am proud of Andrea. She has been a joy to work with. She has kept notes and continues to evolve. Her business model has changed and she has branched out to the personal coaching sphere. When I see her hit a bump in the road she has already analyzed and taken action to correct her path.

Story # 26 – My biggest Tip

I have been asked hundreds of times about this. I have to admit working for tips wasn't even on my mind when I received this tip.

I had just started my family's non-profit we named it *Operation Abundance.* It was a Saturday, and I was helping a friend move a fifth wheel trailer.

My friend didn't have very good people skills, and before we arrived at the address he told me that the guy at the house would talk my ear off if I gave him a chance. Upon his request and against my nature I didn't say a word. That is, until it was time to go.

We had hooked up the fifth wheel and we were ready to leave when my friend's prostate kicked in, and he asked to use the man's bathroom.

Since we had a few minutes and it wasn't like me to just stare into space I asked the man one simple question?

I had learned from my friend that this man was an

expert bee handler.

So I asked him, "What can you teach me about bees in ten minutes or less?" His eyes lit up, and he almost ripped the door off of my truck. Before I knew it we were at a dead run through his property.

He showed me what kind of wood to use and how to build a bee box. He taught me the difference between a nine and twelve frame box, besides the obvious three frames. He talked about all the different kinds of bees and their different jobs.

Then he said, "If you take what I've just taught you and you build 1000 bee boxes I will give you the bees to fill those boxes, and I will help you with the contracts to place them in the Almond and Orange groves of California."

The value of that gift was $50,000 for the bees alone. The contracts for the pollination fees are $120,000 a year. The honey is worth another $40,000 a year.

Summary

Yes, I attribute this to my people skills and all that I have learned in the service industry. Without thinking and expecting anything in return I asked a simple question.

That question spoke volumes to that man. I had asked about the love of his life, and I cared to know the answer. I took interest in what interested him. He could tell this not only by my words but also by my countenance, and what he saw in my eyes.

Without so much as a handshake, he gave me all this and never questioned whether I deserved it.

Story # 27 – "Sir, this is a very complicated system, you wouldn't understand.

Everyone says that the phone companies have the worst customer service in the world. In some cases I agree. I have two stories.

In 1988 there were no cell phones. Sprint was trying to bust into the long distance reseller market with their FoN card.

It was kind of like a prepaid phone card. Anyway, I was out of town and on a tight budget. I was in California trying to raise money for a project.

I had talked to a dentist that wanted to put money into our project. All I had to do was call him in the morning and arrange to pickup a check.

The next morning I tried to call him and was rerouted to a call center. I was told that my card was disabled because there was a 100,000-minute phone call on the card and they needed to collect payment before my card could be reinstated.

I told them that the card had worked perfectly less than 12 hours earlier. The girl on the other end of the line informed me that the call in question had happened since then.

I then pulled out a calculator and did the math for the girl.

"12X60 = 720 minutes since my last call"

"100000minutes / 60minutes in a hour = 1,666.666 hours. This can not happen in 720 minutes or 12 hours.".... no response from the operator.

"1666.666hours / 24hours = 69 days cannot happen in 720 minutes or 12 hours"... at this point the operator hung up on me.

To say the least I was livid. I dialed back and believe it or not I got the same operator. I immediately asked to talk to her supervisor. *Her supervisor* told me the same thing, and I told her the math and added, "two months and eight days could not have happened in the last 12 hours".

At this point the supervisor told me it was a *very technical system* and *that you wouldn't understand.*

Never have I been so mad during a phone call.

I have worked on 40 million dollar aircraft in the Air Force, and I don't care if the sub station is on Pluto, and the call is routed through two wormholes. A 69-day phone call cannot fit into a 12-hour period!

I then asked to be transferred to another supervisor. I was promptly transferred to another supervisor. At first I was relieved it was a man. He told me he could see that both of the girls were mistaken. My elation only lasted a split-second, and then I was smacked in the head with more bitter disappointment.

"It wasn't a 100,000 minute phone call, it was a 1,000,000 phone call." My new tormenter informed me.

I quickly went trough the math, $1,000,000 / 60 = 16,666.666$ hours

$16,666.666$ hours $/ 24$ hours in a day $= 694.444$ days
694.444 days $/ 365$ days in a years $= 1$ year and 11

months.

He stopped me and apologized for the mistake and issued me a new card.

As I was hanging up the call he called out to me. Reluctantly, I put the phone back up to my ear, and he told me that when I received the bill that I could go ahead and disregard it.

Summary

Never argue with the customer.

Never hang up on a customer.

Never tell a customer it is too technical, and that they wouldn't understand.

Isn't it ironic that *phone* companies are the ones with the worst phone skills?

You never know who is on the other end of the phone line. It could be a Nuclear Scientist, a Noble Prize Winner, or just an Idiot Savant leaning far to the Idiot side, and he may know how to use a calculator!

Story # 28 – Sprint makes it all right

Sixteen years later.

I have had to fly to Reno, Nevada to be with my wife who had been in a catastrophic car accident. Her mother and one of our twin daughters died. My wife had sustained numerous life threatening injuries.

I am in Reno for weeks, and I have left our other seven children farmed out with family and friends back in Salt Lake City. To make matters worse, I am trying to keep my business afloat over the phone.

At the end of the month I realize that my bill is due in a day or two. So, I call Sprint's customer care to see what can be done. Nervously, I recall the last customer service experience I had with a Sprint operator as I listen to the ringing.

The gentleman that answers listens to my story and looks up my account. I am 5,000 minutes over my plan. I laugh out loud nervously, and comment that I have almost melted my phone since I have used it so much.

He asks if he can put me on hold. I expect the worst. After only a few moments, he comes back, and informs me that Sprint has authorized him to erase the 7,000 minutes, my 2,000 regular minutes, and the 5,000 extra minutes. He also credits me with an extra 5,000 minutes for the next month, and to call if I need help the next month after that.

He also collects the address where I am and sends me a brand new phone.

Summary

I think the policies of Sprint could have improved in those 20 years. More importantly, this gentleman took responsibility and made things happen, and made them happen fast. He didn't even know about my past with Sprint.

Story # 29 – Aiming to be Mediocre

Out of all the lessons I was taught in my career this one is the one that still baffles me.

About the tenth year I had been driving, we had three drivers that had been with the company three or four years. They had put in their time and risen up through the ranks to make it to the day shift.

I wasn't impressed by any of them. They slept in and missed runs among other things. The start of this season was different, each of the previous years they had started strong but fizzled out during the season. This year they started out with poor attitudes from the very beginning.

To make a long story short, they had decided that the way to compete with me, and what I was making was to drag me down to their level.

How they did this was to constantly complain about me to the boss. They included one of the dispatchers in their sinister plan. They would go to the owner and supervisor complaining that I was bribing dispatchers to get better runs.

For one hundred days straight they worked **not** to offer better service or even to make more money, but only to bring me down a few notches in my own ranking. Since we all made the same % in commissions it made no sense to me.

By the end of the season I was exhausted. For the first time ever I almost didn't finish the ski season. At the end of the season party when one of the other drivers who usually came in 2nd or 3rd was announced as the top revenue earner, these three dead beats erupted in celebration.

Summary

Now I am sure there are some that read this and think, "Man this guy is a sore loser". I admit it I hate to lose.

But what did they have to celebrate? They made no more money that year than any other year. They were still the lowest paid day shift drivers in the company. What did they have to celebrate? Another 13th, 14th, 15th place finish.

The funny thing to me is the difference in revenue that year was less than $100. 1st and 2nd place both set personal records and made more money for the company than we had ever made before.

So even though these three didn't move one spot in the rankings and didn't put any more money in their own bank accounts, they got dropdown drunk in their celebration over dragging me down one position.

Mike, Lynn, and Thayne as well as *The Derelict* this book is not for you. Save your money, I don't believe you can be taught.

Story # 30 – The Les Clefs d'Or

I recently had the privilege to interview Ms. Barbara Robert with the Grand America Hotel. In the fall of 2010 she was recognized as the first Utah Native to be accepted as a member of the Les Clefs d'Or (pronounced lay-clay-door) International Concierge Society.

During the interview it was obvious that she loved her position at the Grand America and loved being of service.

As we talked *shop* it was evident that she had an attention to detail and a great memory. She is truly a great *servant* and doesn't think this work is below her in anyway.

At the same time, she looks out for all those in her charge. She will not allow the staff at the Grand America to be abused by another member of the staff, or even more impressive, by any of the hotel guests. In this industry this is very refreshing.

Problem solving is an area where she thrives. Her favorite words are, "I have an awkward request," gives her the ability to spring into action. She takes pride in finding a solution that will satisfy her guests.

Again, in the stories she related, her attention to detail, her great memory, and the fact that she takes ownership of the problems put in front of her are just some of the distinct reasons I can see why she has received this award.

Barbara is a very humble servant. She is happy that she received this award and honored to be recognized by her peers. At the same time, she knows that an award doesn't offer service.

Time management is also something that jumped out at me. When I was driving and I was asked, "How long till we arrive at the airport?" my passengers would laugh at my exactness when I would answer to the minute. Without thinking I almost always was right on.

Just as I arrived to the interview with Ms. Roberts I checked the time. I was fifteen minutes early. She had told me that she could give me an hour for my interview. She came down to meet me immediately. Our time passed quickly, and we both sensed when the interview time was over, neither of us wanting to look rude to the other by looking at our watches.

As I was leaving I checked the time. One hour and one minute had passed.

Summary

Rising to the top of your field is never a fluke. Barbara Roberts loves her job, loves being of service, and loves a challenge. It is obvious in her countenance, in her attention to detail, and her memory.

I enjoyed the time we had for the interview, and I wish her all the success in the world. I am sure she will happy in all she applies herself to.

Story # 31 – Greg

Greg was a new driver. Almost as soon as he started driving for us, our office started getting complaint calls.

His passengers said that he drove too fast, and that they did not feel safe.

As his supervisor I had to tell him to slow down, but the complaints kept coming. I really liked Greg, but after the third complaint I was told to let him go.

Greg was super polite, and I could not figure that he would disregard all the reprimands that I had given him.

Before I let him go I gave him one more chance. I gave him my manifest, climbed into the back of the van, and posed as one of his customers.

Man! I was in fear for my life before we had even left the parking lot!

It wasn't that he drove fast. In fact, just the opposite

was the case. He pulled across traffic so slow I almost screamed out loud thinking the on coming traffic was going to smash into us! He cut corners too sharp, and made lane changes that as a passenger threw you from side to side.

Once we dropped off his true passengers, who looked like they had just ridden the scariest rollercoaster in the world, I immediately took control of the van. To be honest, his passengers including me all looked like *Bill the Cat* from the Opus comic strip.

Summary

As soon as his passengers were out of earshot I talked to him about his driving. He had no idea how bad it was until I had him sit in the back, and I showed him the difference in our techniques.

Greg was focusing on one thing, his speed. He was oblivious to everything else. Being laser focused has its place, but in the service industry you should be able to juggle a few things at a time.

It should be your quest to offer the best service possible. Always be looking ahead. Be aware of your surroundings.

Greg learned to be a good driver for our company. If he can do it anyone can. I truly believe this.

Story # 32 – Senator Sam Nunn

During the 2002 Winter Olympics I was given the assignment to drive for Coca- Cola. Twenty-four drivers were assigned to this account. Coca-Cola didn't want supervisors assigned because they wanted to watch us for a few days before the Olympics so that they could determine whom they wanted in supervisory positions.

When all was said and done they split us into two groups. Fourteen drivers were appointed to drive the guests of Coca- Cola, and ten of us were assigned to drive the VIP's.

Then after two days I was put in charge of both groups as well as being assigned to personally drive the top executives with Coca-Cola and their personal guests. I ended up driving Warren Buffet, Senator Sam Nunn, Evander Holyfield, as well as Mr. Dyson, Mr. Daft, and Mr. Dunn, the top three with Coca-Cola.

Toward the end of the Olympics I had dropped off my passengers at the ski jumping finals. I was standing by waiting for the event to finish when I saw Senator Nunn walking back alone. I jumped out of the van and let him in. I ran around the van and asked if I needed to take him back to the hotel. He said it wasn't necessary, that he didn't want to cause any unnecessary trouble. Even though I assured him it was no trouble, he was content to wait for the others and warm up in the van.

Then he surprised me. "May I ask you a question?"

"Of course" I answered.

He continued, "Why are you doing this? Lee, I have been watching you. You have not been intimidated by anyone I have seen you come in contact with. You have talked economics with Mr. Buffet, sports and boxing with Mr. Holyfield, business with three of the most powerful business leaders in the world; Dyson, Daft, and Dunn, and politics with a U. S. Senator". He continued, "Even a Senator from the *other side* of the aisle." He joked, "I have thoroughly enjoyed our conversations." And again he asked, **"Why are you doing this?"**

My answer to him was "Sir, I never finished my senior year of high school. I enjoy being of service to people, I have found that I am good at it, and that I can make good money doing it." Then I told him, "Sir, I am able to make a $3,500 paycheck every two weeks and in addition to that I average the same in tips." He stopped me as he did the math.

" Did you just say you make $14,000 a month in commissions and tips combined?! That is more than some doctors bring home. I apologize for my assumptions."

Summary

There was no apology necessary. I wasn't offended. I think he actually gave me a huge complement, as well as his true concern for what I was doing with my life.

One of the reasons I wanted to write this book is to show that the sky is the limit. Service industry *jobs* are considered to be dead end jobs. I think I have proven that they don't need to be.

They are a great opportunity to learn and sharpen your skills. Every business is in the customer service industry, and everyone in the company needs to have great customer service skills, starting at the top.

Every endeavor I have been in since, I have used what I learned while I was in the service industry.

I believe that starting out in the service industry is a chance to build your entrepreneurial skills at no cost to you. As a driver I was able to brand myself by the service that I provided. I was able to test philosophies and approaches so that I now know the value of each of them.

Story # 33 – The Best Waitress in History

My wife will be excited that I decided to include this story.

It was evident Andrea was a great waitress immediately. She greeted us with a smile and engaged us from the moment we sat down in her section at the Olive Garden.

I'm sure when we first started talking none of us could have predicted what was going to happen. Andrea found out we were there for our anniversary. Also, that our baby sitter had cancelled on us at the last second. Well looking back, actually one of our sitters had cancelled. We had five children, all boys, and we had arranged a sitter for the four oldest, and another one for the baby. The one for the baby was the sitter that cancelled.

Her interrogation didn't stop there. She also was able to ascertain that I had visited Italy for five months on two different trips.

As it turned out, she was from Sardinia, an Italian island below Corsica. It so happened that Sardinia was the base from which I was able to see most of Italy.

She also found that while there I caught an octopus while snorkeling in the Mediterranean Sea just off a beach of Sardinia. We were able to take that octopus to a restaurant that we ate at almost every night, and the owner cooked it for us for dinner.

Even sitting here right now I can't believe she did all this interrogation without my wife or I feeling the least bit intruded upon.

She did this on a busy night when all her tables were full.

As a matter of fact, one of the other couples at the next table commented to us that they came to this Olive Garden just for the service that Andrea offered.

Summary

Olive Garden knew the value of Andrea. I know this beyond a shadow of a doubt because I told them. In my conversation with the manager he told me at least once a night he gets a raving review for Andrea.

Andrea knows her worth and the worth of great service. I have had her sit with my wife and I and talked to her about it.

She has branded herself and her over the top service. Olive Garden has benefited from this branding. Many times I have called ahead to make sure we had a table in her section. Some of those times I have agreed to wait longer just to make sure we were seated in her section.

Andrea even offered to come to our home one anniversary to make her favorite recipe, Octopus ink soup.

Story # 34 – Who's the Boss

One of my favorite house accounts was for a very gracious celebrity. He had a beautiful home in Deer Valley.

Most of his guests were from New York and needed to be picked up at 4o'clock in the morning to be able to make the flight back to New York. He requested that he have the same driver if at all possible. I was given this assignment. After proving myself a number of times I was invited to come in and wait for the guest instead of waiting in the van, each time he had a hot cup of coffee just the way I liked it.

Summary

In the beginning I would see him giving his guest the tip money. As I proved myself, the tip was put on the tray that he served my coffee on.

Even though he was the *boss* he wasn't afraid to serve a servant. I truly miss serving him and his family.

He sold his Deer Valley home after he was involved in a terrible skiing accident. I am not sure if he would remember these four in the morning acts of kindness, but I still do.

Story # 35 – Never have a Bad Day

This is a very extreme story, but I truly believe **if I can do it anyone can.**

The 2003/2004-ski season was the hardest season for me to return to driving. Just after the 2002/2003-ski season had ended my wife had a catastrophic car accident. We lost one of our twins in that accident just a week before they were to turn one year old. We also lost my wife's mother. To say the least we were devastated both emotionally and financially. Without going into to much detail it was a very tough time for our family.

Summary

I needed to pull our family out of ruin. I realized quickly that even though I tried to mask my depression, my clients could pick up on what I was thinking. I had to make an effort to be happy, not just pretend to be happy. Before I knew it I was getting through my day without remembering how terrible the horizon looked. I learned that no matter how bad it looked, just beyond what we could see, there were always clear skies coming.

Even though I started out slower than ever, I was able to over come a slow start and finish better than I ever had.

Story # 36 – Satan is Calling

Some business owners will not like this story, but here it is anyway.

Eight months before the Olympics were to start everyone that was going to be with the company was invited to a meeting.

At that meeting we were told what the pay would be, and that any of us who wanted to pursue other options it wouldn't be held against those of us who chose to pursue those options.

Some left for that reason. Those of us who stayed were promised a contract. Month after month no contract was signed.

Finally the night before we were to start driving was upon us, and again the owner was a no show for the driver meeting.

I had just gotten a new phone, and was busy programming numbers into it when I came to the owner of the company that I was to drive for. In my discouraged state, instead of his name I replaced it with Satan.

To say the least, only hours before the Olympics were to start my boss and I were at odds. All the drivers were distraught and thinking that the owner had duped us yet again.

The temporary drivers he brought in had told us that night what they were being paid, and it was half of what was promised.

I pulled all of the drivers that had been promised the contract into our own private meeting. The general thought was that we would have to take what was given.

My feeling was that if we allowed the owner to get away with this we would continue to have our pay erode year after year. My plan was to all report to work at the appointed time, 3 a.m. But we were to stand together and agree not to put our vans into gear until a contract was produced. The agreement was made, and we all went home to get a good night sleep before we all reported to our vans.

At 1 a.m. the next morning the ringing of my phone awakened my wife and me.

My wife was the one that stumbled across the bedroom and reached the phone first. I asked her who it was, and without even missing a beat she told me it was Satan.

She handed me my phone, and slipped back into bed as I answered the call.

Satan tore right into me. "Who do you think you are?" He screamed. "I hear that you are trying to organize the drivers against me."

I calmly explained to the *Dark One* that we were only interested in what we had been promised. He threatened to fire me on the spot but I knew he was on contract to have every van on the road, so I stood my ground. The dealing began.

Satan snarled, "I will give you the contract for the price I promised, but only you." Then he hung up.

Me having the direct number to Satan, I called him back, and told him that I needed to make sure all of the drivers that were promised the rate would get what they were promised, or none of us would move our vans one inch.

Satan screamed into the phone, "I'll give you twice the amount I promised if you agree to get those vans on the road, as long as nobody knows what I gave you!!!" And again he hung up.

Again, I called him back and told him that I needed to make sure all of the drivers that were promised the rate would get what they were promised, or none of us would move our vans one inch.

Finally with much gnarling and gnashing of teeth, Satan agreed to fulfill the contract. I agreed to have all the drivers start their days as if nothing was wrong with the agreement, that we would have contracts in hand by noon that first day.

Summary

I cannot stress the importance of integrity. Even if I had accepted Satan's 2nd offer, I would have had to sleep with myself. And as Satan tried by design to derail me, during the next few month's, things were always made right by forces greater than him or I.

My wife commented that she couldn't believe she had witnessed her husband, in his underwear, dealing with Satan himself right there in her bedroom.

Story # 37– Kerry Brown

The first day I met Kerry I was impressed. He is a Jolly Soul and a pleasure to be around.

Kerry did his own analysis before coming to work with us. He had watched us before he came to work, and watched and learned from me and the other top drivers after he was hired. He soon became one of the top drivers.

Kerry has a laugh that is infectious, and he has a great personality. His customers enjoyed every minute they were in his care. Consistently his passengers raved about him to me.

Summary

I liken the ski season to the Iditarod. In this analogy the drivers are the sled dogs. All great sled dogs need more than just leaders. They need those that can replace the lead dog at a moments notice. Bryan, Norm, and one old dog whose name escapes me, were always right there nipping at my heels. An act I see and appreciate that made me better. It made us all better.

Kerry is a workhorse and a leader in the making along with Mike Wilhelm.

Derrick is the dog you decide to cut lose quickly. He doesn't pull in the right direction, and just doesn't get it. He will ruin any team you try to put him with.

Mike, Lynn, and Thayne are the dogs that do just enough not to be cut loose, and you might as well keep them around in case you need a fur coat or protein in an emergency.

Story # 38 – The Exact Value of a Smile

It's nice to be smiled at – and we can now put an exact price on each grin we give, thanks to a new study carried out in Wales. But sadly it's not a quick route to riches: a smile is worth exactly one-third of a penny sterling, or $0.43.

I did not include this earlier, but I was asked so many times, as I had people proof this book, if smiling was important. Of course it is. I overlooked the obvious things like smiling, wearing deodorant, wearing clean and pressed clothes, looking your guests in the eye, and speaking clearly and politely. All these things and are important.

Please, if you find something not included in this small book, don't think that if it is not included it is not important.

This study is very interesting to me. I am not a smiley person. I have to force myself to smile. Some people call me a *Deep Thinker,* but the truth is I forget to smile.

This is so much the case that I have the persona of being a mean or grumpy person.

I have learned that people are always watching. So smile! They will assume the best instead of the worst.

Summary

During my career one of the standards that we shot for was to move one hundred people in a day. At 43 cents per transaction I now wonder how much money I left on the table because I forgot to smile?

Bonus Video Stories

The next five videos are stories I have found while researching the web to see if there was a need for this book.

Links are included to videos so these stories can be told in the presenter's own words. I hope they help drive home the importance of great service.

Scott McKain tells this first story. A Story about a #1) Cab Driver named "Taxi Terry".

#2) This gentleman tells his "Wendy Story"

#3) Ross Shafer turns into an unpaid spokesperson for "Maria Garcia"

#4) Shep Hyken tells his story about an "Outstanding Cab Driver"

#5) Barbara Glanz tells her story about "Johnny the Bagger"

Summary

If a couple Taxicab Drivers, a Airline Boarding Agent, a Room Service Associate, a Grocery Store Bagger with Downs Syndrome, and a Shuttle Driver can figure out what they need to do to offer great, outstanding Service, I believe anyone can.

More importantly, in this financial climate we had better figure it out. From the top to the bottom every company needs to focus and understand Customer Service.

Scott McKain spends the first thirty-seven seconds of his video talking about the bad reputation of Delta Airlines. As business owners we need to make sure our customers aren't doing the same about our companies. If we have a bad reputation we need to do everything in our power to reverse the publics view of our company.

At the same time, as employees we need to build customer loyalty to the companies we represent and at the same time build loyalty to ourselves.

Is the Service Industry Right for You?

Only you can determine that. For me I have loved being of service to others. I hope to be of service all of my life.

For those of you that want to give the best service possible, I hope this book has been of service to you. The more you put into service the more you will get back. It will prepare you for any endeavor that you decide to take on.

I hope that this book can provide the spark and education that you need to thrive in this industry. Whether it is as a Driver, Waitress, Bellman, Salesman, Small business owner, Head of a Corporation, and everything in-between. Maybe even a Les Clefs d'Or or two.

Service is the key that will propel you to the front of the pack.

In whatever I do I want to be the leader of the pack,

because the leader sets the pace. I thrive when the dogs behind me are nipping at my heels, but the key here is to offer service at the same time.

I do not know how many times I have slowed down and even stopped so that I can offer better service to the customer that is with me at the time instead of hurrying them out of my van.

Every time I have done this it had been the right thing to do, and I have benefited each and every time.

Resources or Links

My wife pointed out that some people might purchase a physical copy of this book. Interesting concept!

To contact me about the information in this book email me at Lee@tipsontipsbook.com

Follow our blog at http://www.tipsontipsbook.com

Here are the addresses to the videos

Taxi Terry

http://www.youtube.com/watch?v=7XNFYBB1j Q&NR=1

Wendy Story

http://www.youtube.com/watch?v=JPrpzODobw 0&NR=1

Maria Garcia

http://www.youtube.com/watch?v=8T54rQrMle A&feature=related

Outstanding Cab Driver

http://www.youtube.com/watch?v=YG48U5iPES
A&feature=related

Johnny the Bagger

http://www.youtube.com/watch?v=qOZPlt3Ha0
Y

*